Ripples in the Fabric of the Universe

Ripples in the Fabric of the Universe

new & selected
poems

Jim Tilley

Red Hen Press | *Pasadena, CA*

Book design by Mark E. Cull

Library of Congress Cataloging-in-Publication Data

Names: Tilley, Jim, author.
Title: Ripples in the fabric of the universe: new & selected poems / Jim
  Tilley.
Other titles: Ripples in the fabric of the universe (Compilation)
Description: First edition. | Pasadena, CA: Red Hen Press, 2024.
Identifiers: LCCN 2023038550 (print) | LCCN 2023038551 (ebook) | ISBN
  9781636281452 (paperback) | ISBN 9781636281490 (hardcover) | ISBN
  9781636281506 (e-book)
Subjects: LCGFT: Poetry.
Classification: LCC PS3620.I515 R57 2024 (print) | LCC PS3620.I515
  (ebook) | DDC 811/.6—dc23/eng/20230913
LC record available at https://lccn.loc.gov/2023038550
LC ebook record available at https://lccn.loc.gov/2023038551

The National Endowment for the Arts, the Los Angeles County Arts Commission, the Ahmanson Foundation, the Dwight Stuart Youth Fund, the Max Factor Family Foundation, the Pasadena Tournament of Roses Foundation, the Pasadena Arts & Culture Commission and the City of Pasadena Cultural Affairs Division, the City of Los Angeles Department of Cultural Affairs, the Audrey & Sydney Irmas Charitable Foundation, the Meta & George Rosenberg Foundation, the Albert and Elaine Borchard Foundation, the Adams Family Foundation, Amazon Literary Partnership, the Sam Francis Foundation, and the Mara W. Breech Foundation partially support Red Hen Press.

First Edition
Published by Red Hen Press
www.redhen.org

ACKNOWLEDGMENTS

Providing poets and writers a home for their work is a true gift—I cannot thank Kate Gale and Mark Cull, founders of Red Hen Press, enough for giving me that.

Many thanks to Rick Campbell and James Scruton for their constructive suggestions on revisions to various drafts of many of these poems.

Also a hearty thank you to my wife and literary agent, Deborah Schneider, who nudged me to transform many of these poems into more powerful pieces, sometimes against my initial resistance, but always gratefully accepted in the end.

I am especially grateful to the journals and magazines that chose to publish the following poems, sometimes in earlier versions and under different titles.

Atlanta Review: "Painting"; *BigCityLit.com*: "The Graph of You"; *Café Review*: "Gale-Force Winds"; *California Quarterly*: "Cranberry Fields Forever," "Ripples in the Fabric of the Universe"; *Chronogram*: "Milkweed and Beech," "Safe Harbor," "Ode to a Golfer"; *Cider Press Review*: "Outdoor Fire"; *Eunoia Review*: "Cairn," "He Could Still See the Light," "Bare Branches"; *Evening Street Review*: "Stalking Prey," "When a Hydrant Is Blue," "Someone's God Somewhere"; *Front Range Review*: "The Place You'd Call Home"; *Glimpse Poetry Magazine*: "Transfixed in a Waltz"; *Grey Sparrow Journal*: "Child Coloring in a War Zone"; *Hawai'i Pacific Review*: "Unable to See Our Way Clear"; *I-70 Review*: "Return to Oia," "Stopping by Woods," "The Town in Its Wisdom Cuts Our Trees"; *Kestrel*: "Gardening"; *Midwest Quarterly Review*: "Why I Prefer Numbers to Words"; *New Feathers Anthology*: "Acorns Falling on Our Heads"; *North Dakota Quarterly*: "Handing Down"; *Oberon Magazine*: "Unsung Hymn During the Time of Covid"; *Poetry South*: "And Still the Earth is Shaking," "Channeling Plato"; *Stone Poetry Quarterly*: "It's Time to Talk," "The Two Owls"; *Studio One*: "Whiteface Mountain"; *Tar River Poetry*: "Goatland"; *Third Wednesday*: "On the Merits of Taking Up Pickleball," "You Choose to Die in Your Bed"; *Tipton Poetry Journal*: "The Bell"; and *Weber—The Contemporary West*: "White Pond."

in memory of my parents, Betty and Don,

and for my two sons, Jack and Brad

CONTENTS

from
IN CONFIDENCE
2011

from
CRUISING AT SIXTY TO SEVENTY
2014

from

LESSONS FROM SUMMER CAMP

2016

NEW POEMS

from

IN CONFIDENCE

2011

Murmur

Every fall and spring, we drove
to Boston to let the doctors

poke and listen, jelly our chests
for electrocardiograms.

We always stayed at the same hotel,
swam laps in the indoor pool

the night before the tests,
my son's brazen show of force

to warn whichever god was watching
that his valve worked well,

the time for carving far away.
He'd float on his back listening

for the telltale echo, backwash
against a background wash of waves,

and ask if I could hear it too.
Then he'd want to race—

one final churning length
to end this leg of the journey—

so tired afterward he'd fall asleep
before I could say goodnight.

One spring I went to Boston
alone, and returned

with a six-inch scar
to match his. He showed me

how to clutch a pillow
when I laughed, and made me

laugh hard, warned that an elephant
like his pink and grey one

would sit on my chest
for three months, then gloated

when I had six months of the same
headaches I was certain

he'd invented just for sympathy.
And as he got his first

true migraine, we compared
our blue-and-white lightning-bolt

auras that bring on splitting pain
and the clearest vision one can imagine.

HALF-FINISHED BRIDGE

No important work to do today, I think,
as I lie in the hammock one last time
before storing it for winter,
just a few chores around the yard—
deck chairs to be stacked and stashed away
and the lawn raked despite the pears
and oaks hanging on to their green.

Stamped on the pencil I'm using,
first snow falling on the half-finished bridge,
now as in Bashō's time,
the halfway done possibly a road
to nowhere, like the wars we shouldn't start
and the marriages we can't finish.
But he must've meant that I find myself

amidst the season's first flurries,
leaves collecting at my feet
as I rock in the wind, writing to my father
that I'm grateful he's still alive
and there's time to erect the rest of the trestle
and walk together to the other side,
light snow falling on our backs.

Binoculars

I set aside the paper with its front-page notice
        about Updike's death
and saw my son staring out the window
        past the fence to where a large bird
pecked at the ground, beak flecked with red and sticky

        bits of fur. On the ground a dead rabbit,
what else could it have been?
        Then another bird, the first still picking
at the carcass, the second standing still,
        wings spread full, marking the spot for others,

waiting its turn. Wild turkeys, he said,
        but as I looked through the binoculars,
I could see the markings weren't right—
        they were vultures and their fare
a six-point buck on its side in the snow,

        an eye gouged out, a rib snapped in half
as if from a blow, right hind leg
        gnawed to the bone. Then three birds,
one eating, two waiting, each knowing
        its place. Okay, this is a good place

to admit I couldn't find the binoculars.
        While the bird was busy feasting,
I had walked out to the fence
        to perform the autopsy, and while I was
curious about the decorum in the queue,

it was the bright red blood
pooled between the bare ribs that gripped me—
        how the color of life
can still inhabit the non-living,
        a relationship show signs of life

though its ribs are broken
        and its unseen eye no longer glistens.
Always the lingering question
        about the cause of death and its precise time,
the disembodied sense of staring at oneself

        and not recognizing the creature.
How you can't know when you're actually dead,
        though you must have felt it.
And that is where it always expires—
        the metaphor out there in the snow.

You turn away and walk back to the house
        of your life, up to where
someone still stands at the window. And whatever
        happened out there, you'll say you were
both right: they were turkey vultures.

Chemotherapy

From the window she can see the breeze
riffle the forsythia's yellow spray,
and near the willow, her favorite magnolia,
a pointillistic pink-and-white pastel
not yet painted over by leaves.

Sometime between the wind taking
no note of bare branches
and the forest hiding behind its green,
her apple trees will become giant
dandelions gone to seed.

In this fragile equilibrium, an ether
between too many and too few,
she lies down beside her sleeping lover
to stroke his back, and almost forgets
about this time next year.

EMPTY CASINGS

> *The empty shell casings*
> *are not worth anything to us.*
> —Lt. Gary Gallinot,
> spokesperson, Santa Monica PD

My friend looked surprised when I gave him
a Cambodian peace bell for Hanukkah
    and told him what it was, tiny copper chime
that villagers make for their oxen
    by melting down exploded landmines,
striving to transmute their heritage of swords.

    I hadn't seen him in over a year, not since
his son's bar mitzvah. I'm not a Jew,
    haven't heard the story again and again
of so much light from so little oil.
    Didn't grow up learning how many olives
one has to press, unlike the children

    of the Bais Chabad synagogue in Santa Monica
making menorahs from the empty casings
    of their PD's target practice. My friend
will soon learn more than he wants to know
    about target practice, about rearing a child
as spent bullets collect on both sides,

    mother unable to wean herself from the son,
father retreating into work and travel.
    He will learn about the landmines in divorce,

will see how much light can come
       from the last oil of a marriage.
How hard he's finding it to press the olives,

       how hard to reclaim his heritage, his mother's
fine china passed down from her mother
       and the family brass-and-copper menorah
made by German POWs in an Allied camp
       where his father had kept them hard at work
melting down the empty casings of a war.

STATE OF THE UNION

You might have thought they were talking
about how to fix the broken economy
after the bubble burst, years of squawking
about who's really the enemy,
Party A and Party B in full dispute
about the need for intervention,
her monetary policy the root
of their issues and she with no intention
of getting it under control, a grim
situation with no sign of what could
lead to recovery and no idea who
would help to set things straight, just a dim
recollection by each of having once stood
face to face solemnly saying "I do."

In Spring, Mathematics Are Yellow

I'm sure there's something fractal
        in forsythia, not so much its chaotic sprays,
which are probably not parabolic curves
        (and certainly not catenaries
hanging under the weight of blossoms),

        but the contours of the bush, branch and flower
that are shaped like a year in my life
        or its day or hour. Up close, I can see
each bloom has four petals, thus proving
        the limits of Fibonacci's reach,

his long arm able to paint five
        on the pansies I potted for my wife, but not
across the street where our neighbor buried
        perennial memories of his wife ten years ago.
How odd never to have seen the daffodils

        as hexagrams before. They die too soon,
unlike the dandelions that dot my yard—
        too many to fight, yet finite, unlikely Fibonacci,
though undoubtedly fractal (or so Mandelbrot
        would claim), always inappropriate

for bouquets of reconciliation, firmly rooted
        in the life of my lawn, while the lawn of my life
goes to seed faster than an exponential plot,
        and all the quantized fluff
tunnels into next year's plans, like it or not.

The Big Questions

The big questions are big only
because they have never been answered.
Some questions, big as they seem,
are big only in the moment,
like when you're hiking a trail alone

and you encounter a mammoth
grizzly who hasn't had lunch
in a fortnight, and he eyes you
as the answer to his only big question.
Life turns existential, and you can't

help questioning why you are here—
in this place on this planet
within this universe—
at this precise time,
or why he is, and you know he's not,

even for a moment, wondering
the same thing, because he's already
figured it out. And you, too,
know exactly what to do.
So, this can be a defining moment,

but not a big question,
because no one ever figures those out.
Still, one day when someone does,
might it not be a person like you
staring down a bear looking for lunch?

Richter 7.8

Dark energy and dark matter describe proposed solutions
to as yet unresolved gravitational phenomena. So far as
we know, the two are distinct.

—Robert Caldwell, cosmologist,
SciAm.com, August 28, 2006

Such a waste to spend a life thinking
about the impossible to figure out, like where the spirit
goes when detached from its body.

An alternate universe perhaps. That's where
dark matter enters, not how physicists hypothesize,
but the way it casts light on everyday affairs.

I, for one, am stuck on the question
of how dark matter and energy can be separate and distinct
when plain mass and energy are equivalent.

We're told we need both types of darkness
to fill what's missing, yet one pulls us together
while the other propels us apart.

What we can't find in our world must be
the substance of another,
worlds that look to each other for what's missing,

each a resting place for the other's souls,
an answer to why any god would allow a quake
to bury nine hundred children under a school,

what's so incomprehensible here on earth
maybe making sense in the place where all those students
have found new flesh to wear.

Serendipity in the Cosmos

I could try to deal with the big question
of why any of us is present in this universe,
but that would cause me to set aside
the immediate matter of why I was absent

from my bedroom yesterday afternoon,
not reclining against the pillows as I
usually am, reading poetry before I succumb
to the warmth of the late-day sun.

It would also force me to shelve the questions
of why my son took up golf at age four,
why we bought this Tudor house
fourteen years ago, with a lawn barely

large enough for a full wedge shot, yet far too
vast to maintain ourselves, and how we found
our immigrant gardener of ten years,
whose men forever struggle against the tug

of their mowing machines with spinning blades
that occasionally catch a stray stone
embedded in the rough and sling it as if towards
some unknown enemy who does not realize

his fortune is about to change. It is no small thing
that the workers came this week on Monday
when Tuesday is their usual day,
and in the afternoon instead of morning,

and I have to wonder why, after all the years
his mother told him not to play in the backyard,
my son grabbed a fistful of old Titleist balls
last fall before he returned to college,

still not listening at age twenty-one,
and knocked them back and forth across the lot,
then left them strewn upon the lawn
for a workman to snag as he tilted and turned

the lumbering hulk of his mower. It remains
a mystery how the dimpled projectile managed
to arc its way into the third-story bedroom,
leaving a telltale hole in the pane

of a window normally swung wide open
to let in fresh air, but cranked shut after the April
heat wave broke. Of course, you say,
it is now clear why there was little resistance,

the inside winter storm having been removed,
the summer screen raised, the indoor
shutters not drawn because the sun was not yet
low enough to be blinding, but no one,

not even the muses, can explain why
my ex-wife decided yesterday that it was time
at last to cast off her heavy blanket of loneliness
and have me take some smiling photographs

to post to her friends, thus causing me
to edit her favorite few on the laptop computer
in my office far away from the spray of leaded glass
that showered the spot still cooling

on my pillow where I had left the May issue
of *Poetry* opened up to Jane Hirshfield's
"Assay Only Glimpsable for an Instant," one moment
black and white and then a rainbow of color.

FISH STORY

I couldn't see anything in the eyes
of the spiny brown-and-white striped
blowfish swept far up onto the beach
and left stranded on wet sand sweating
in the sun. I set down my camera,
and peered past the gold rims,

through the lenses and deep into the
dark, primordial wells of the fish,
and it looked back into the same spot
in my being. There we touched,
inner fish to inner fish. In my best
silent fishspeak, I told it there was

a parable, even a higher purpose—
that it had been chosen to show us
things don't always work out,
that one can't always penetrate the foam
or fathom that bubbles in the churn
can suddenly become gaping holes

in the universe's vast underbelly of hope.
Then I stopped, because I could tell
it hadn't understood, or no longer
cared. I could see it felt no empathy
for the rest of us swaddled in froth.
Besides, its spines looked poisonous.

In Confidence

Why does leaning on the rail of a deck
and looking out over layers of hills
as buds burst through their coverings
evoke the big questions? Like why
are we making such a mess of it all?

Ask Sunday's dissonant choir of birds
in the newspaper's Week in Review,
always a replay of the same
failures. Lots of cartoons there
to remind us that making fun of ourselves

is a start but not an end. Take today—
though it could be any day—
a young girl with a bow in her hair
asking her bald-headed ex-VP granddad
to teach her new dog a trick,

so he grasps the pup by its scruff,
and pours a glass of water down its throat
while screaming, Speak! Speak!
I know we should, but it's so hard
to feel tortured out here

watching the oak unfold its leaves.
Besides, waterboarding sounds like
an amusement park ride,
what you might do with your kids
at Typhoon Lagoon. I know I would

give up secrets. That's why
you should never trust me with one,
though I must admit
that your brief affair with a colleague
will always be safe with me.

Folding

I stare blankly at my mother-in-law's longhand
legacy to her daughter, Crisco thumbprints smearing
some of the India ink. My wife's away and my son

waits for his Sunday pancakes as I puzzle over
Fold buttermilk and an egg into the dry ingredients.
No hints, merely a warning. I've learned

that major perils attend misfolding, that proteins
stuck mid-stream, half-folded on the way
to proper states, can transform a normal brain

into bubbly batter with lumps. I've been taught
how to fold laundered shirts and sheets,
items I burn at times while ironing out problems,

but never as badly as the toast I charred today.
I unfold the morning paper, sit down with my black
coffee to digest the Week in Review, and note

as I read about the latest bombings that recipes
don't always turn out right, that sometimes
it may be better to fold, even for the Master Chef.

Boys

My friends and I couldn't buy cherry bombs
on our weekly allowances. We hoped
that plain firecrackers would be enough
to tear off arms and legs, a private's, not ours.
We were the generals—we ran the war,
decided where to plant soldiers in trenches
we sculpted in mounds left by bulldozers
on the construction site. After the flap
about the Curry boy losing an eye,
we imposed a ceasefire for a week.
Then came the all-out surge to do some
serious damage, the kind that requires you
to eat two bowls of cornflakes every day
to build your army from cereal-box toys.

One Would Hope

that life's final moments travel slowly,
quieting the blood and brain and leaving
time enough to hear one's choice of music,
a plucked lute for the teenage boy driving
through a crowded street—barely entering
a Baghdad square to gather his father
from work, talking to his mother about
new friends at school or scoring the winning
goal in a soccer game—when the bursts
of bullets rang. And for the mother
leaning on her son, a lullaby, the one
her mother sang to her, and she to him.
For both of them, one would hope that life
was long enough to hear each other's song.

On the Art of Patience

With a Mozart concerto in the background
and little to do as I waited for the next available associate
       to be with me shortly, I began to comprehend
how one infinity can be larger than another,
       not in the sense of the mathematician
who can prove that rational numbers are countable
       and real numbers are not, but my patience,
which I am continually thanked for,
       the next available associate undoubtedly

unaware of my infinite fascination with Mona Lisa's
       excised eye staring upside down
from the minute hand, obliterating the smile at half past
       the hour on the artisanal timepiece
my wife brought back from Florence last year.
       A larger infinity is what my neighbor's cow
exhibits every day lying near the split-rail fence,
       alone with her thoughts as the cars whoosh by.
This morning, she half sat, watching the sky clear

       after a gauzy, misting rain that Constable
would have captured in a pastoral scene,
       though the cars would have been horses,
and they would likely have been grazing when the sun
       broke through and beat on their backs, the life
of horses not so different from the life of cows
       or people on hold, or even an artist like Reinhardt
whose work seemed to be rushed near the end
       of his life, no doubt the reason

he turned to monochromes and they turned so black,
        the tall rectangles of earlier paintings
ceding their space to smaller squares, the subtle changes
        in hue and tone maybe discernible by others,
but not me, though they might have been
        had I been able to view one at MoMA
under different light and catch a trace
        of the mountains at deep dusk he must first have
brushed onto the canvas, followed by a beach

        with bathers clad only in dark skin, then a black
haystack with Black-Eyed Susans off to the right,
        and ending with a self-portrait that explicated
his choice of color—undetailed, unremitting, permitting,
        no not permitting, but coercing
the viewer's mind to co-exist with the artist's, as in
        stepping into Gaudí's forest of columns
that draw one's eyes to a ceiling where porphyritic trunks
        branch into geometry, the redwood canopy

leaving no sense of outside world, there being no sign
        of anyone's god lurking in the stained glass,
no resolution of apse from transept amidst a thicket
        of rusted iron shafts and crossbeams,
scaffold for the project he couldn't complete in a lifetime,
        that may never be finished in anyone's lifetime
my wife and I concluded as we passed through
        the timelessness of the cathedral on our recent trip
to Barcelona. Finishing is not the point in art,

just calling it quits when one runs out of patience
or some other project commandeers the mind,
        which brings to mind the plight of the pandas,
a species also on hold, who, like their forebear
        Ling Ling, have trouble procreating
in captivity, the problem not that there aren't enough
        bamboo shoots or Eucalyptus leaves
to keep them healthy and amorous, or enough open space
        to tango with a mate,

but unlike the cow trying to insinuate herself
        into the Constable landscape, the female panda
doesn't see the point of lying around
        feigning lack of interest until her consort
springs into action. Or perhaps she can see
        the thing is being filmed and refuses to take part
in panda porn, isn't fooled or moved by Mozart
        saturating the air from speakers hidden in trees,
no more than I was for 19 minutes and 57 seconds

        (no, Mona Lisa doesn't have a second hand,
but the rose-gold Tourneau that my wife
        bought me in New York City does)
kindly continuing to hold for the next available associate
        at William Ashley, sole Canadian distributor
for the English Portmeirion Botanic Garden collection
        of fine china, in particular the six 8"-diameter
pasta bowls featuring the Treasure Flower,
        Eastern Hyacinth, Sweet William, Garden Lilac,

Dog Rose, and Belladonna Lily, their common names.
        Later, with more time, though for no good reason,
I was able to find the Latin appellations,
        which, in the interest of space, I won't provide.
Did I mention that I was trying to buy the pasta bowls
        for my mother's 80th birthday in two weeks' time?
Or that the next available associate told me
        they were out of stock? Would you like
the salad bowls instead? she asked.

SLAYING PHILISTINES

When we are no longer children,
we are already dead.
　　　　— Constantin Brancusi

Perhaps it's a story of happenstance
that begins with a village carpenter
and ends with a master in his dusty atelier,

always the unschooled shepherd
who harbors no ambitions
to lead an army, but dreams
of a magical bird, the mythical Maiastra
lifting him to perch with her
on a boulder at the edge of space
where they'll cajole a falcon's wings to stillness
and wax them with the sun,

or perhaps it's about a boy's hunger
to mold a piece of goat cheese,
whittle branches into wands, massage shavings
between his thumb and fingers, rub toes
against a stream's smooth stones,

for how else can you explain
an old man hunched over
a rhombic block of marble, carving
plainsong into crescendo, chiseling away
the husk, struggling
to liberate a creature's spirit?

FISH AT THE DANCE

You've walked from the gallery
where a bird in space
materialized in the mind
of a peasant boy tending sheep,
featureless bronze buffed to high luster
carved into one long sweeping curve
whose equation he could not fathom,
and now you're swimming the depths
of his ocean, staring at blue-gray
mottled marble—
no tail, no fins, no scales,
no gills, no eyes—
headed for the stairway
where against the landing's wall
five salmon-skinned women
join hand-in-hand in dance,
Matisse's circle not quite closed,
still a spot for Brancusi's creature
making the leap.

Rehearsal

Leaning back in her flamingo-pink crocheted hat
not pulled quite snug, lime green plugs

showing in her ears, glasses tipped a bit
at the end of her nose, her velvet burgundy sleeve

drawn neatly to the elbow to free her wrist,
with each stroke the old woman coaxes the notes

from the page, eighths, sixteenths, thirty-seconds
coming quick, her right hand gliding outward

from her chest as it parts the air, then ceasing
without seeming to, a stilling of the delicate wing,

like an osprey drafting the currents above
her treetop nest, then drawn toward it again,

another ephemeral pause, another featherlike wave
of her right hand away from her breast,

cycling faster, slower, faster, the faint white
wisps outside the window bleaching into the sky's

faded blue denim, as they almost always do
when she's wearing her jeans to play at high altitude,

husband asleep in his leather fauteuil, the four
slightly splayed fingers of her right hand arched

across the absent bow resting on the thumb below,
a ballerina's arm and fingers moving to the score,

her head cocked to the left, her eyes half closed,
each unbroken sweep of her hand lifting a phrase,

she alone in a sound-filled space until she holds
the final note, throat quivering as the piece dissolves.

The air no longer resonant, the music now folded
and put back in its envelope, clasp fastened,

sleeve eased down onto her wrist again, her hat
pulled tight about her ears, her chair snapped back

into its upright pose, glasses pushed up along her
angular nose, eyes glistening in the day's late rays,

her face awash in transient smile, the bird
at rest in her nest, her mate unmoved in his place.

Aluminum Rush

Aluminium et design, Musée des beaux-arts,
Montréal, August 23 to November 4, 2001

You kick back on a serpentine chaise
fashioned from soda-can squares,

soak up the shade of an all-season maple
with leaves that won't rust, stain or peel.

You listen to your favorite heavy metal
played on light-metal guitars

and begin to feel the awesome power
of element #13, the promise of the future.

Before you stands the motorcycle
you've always wanted to own, the essence

of light, reflecting sun that streams
onto the Musée des beaux-arts exhibition.

You imagine hopping aboard and riding
into the heavens, passing Icarus

on his way down to another close encounter
with your high school English teacher,

through the surface of Brueghel's painting
and into the lines of Auden's poem.

You can't help but pity poor Daedalus;
if only he'd known about aluminum,

he could have saved himself a lot of wax
and spared the masters their oils and ink.

FROZEN OVER

Though the reservoir has frozen over,
no fishermen have ventured out to drill
their holes, plumb the bottom. The ice is still
finding its place, relieving pent-up stress
by fracturing, the making of each crack
accompanied by a melancholy
low-pitched moan, always the sound of rending
the whole. The lake won't break up until spring.
Meanwhile, each unruptured sheet's a country
living in fragile peace with its neighbors,
sometimes splitting, a new boundary formed.
There you are standing at the edge, thinking
you have to decide whether to step out
into that world, but you already have.

Not Yet

No, not when you haven't finished counting the new
wrinkled leaves unfolding the oak, taken
last year's sum, then swum that number of laps

in the granite-cold pool before easing into the hot tub
to watch wisps break away from the mothership
and your children cross their thresholds. Not until

you've heard the wind as wishfulness turns to deed.
No matter that your joints have become the first
to greet you in the morning, even before you slip

out of bed, or that you need bifocals for the paper,
hearing aids for the birds. You stay because you want to
know where the ocean will draw the world's waistline

in a hundred years, whether what's left of continents
will come together again or continue to drift apart.
Easy enough, you figure, since you already don't exist

in your former state. Yes, you'll accept the rest
as plastic and titanium, having tried them in your heart.
You just hope they get the brain's circuitboards right.

from

CRUISING AT SIXTY TO SEVENTY

2014

Particle and Wave

particles have no meaning as isolated entities,
but can only be understood as interconnections . . .
—Erwin Schrodinger

You and I were doing what we do best—
throwing stones—
this time from the side
of a country bridge into the reservoir,
each arcing under the forces
of physics until impact, the consequence
spreading in ripples, the stone
become invisible in the bottom muck,
its presence propagating
across the surface,
as our presence does
to the fabric of something less grand
than space-time. Then yours and mine
cast together, landing in different spots,
their wavelets colliding,
passing through each other,
cohering in some places, canceling in others,
the pattern richer for the two
than one . . .   then in our excitement,
each of us tossing a handful at once,
the pattern becoming richer still,
not still at all, moving out into the world—
children, siblings, parents, friends,
adding up to something grand.

Problem #193

It was Banach's wife who gave them the journal
they called *The Scottish Book* so they wouldn't
keep losing the solutions they wrote on the marble
tabletops in the Scottish Café, those famous

mathematicians in Lvov who kept a log
of the solvable and unsolvable, as you do now
in your journal with the marble pattern on its cover.
I've been thinking about Problem #193,

Banach's puzzle involving a mathematician
who carries two boxes of matches,
one in his left pocket and one in his right,
each with M matches at the start. To light his pipe,

he chooses a box at random, removes a match
and strikes it. Does this every time until he finds
one of the boxes is empty. But how would he know?
When he reaches for another match and finds

the box bare? I've been thinking this could be us.
Not the times we're lying in bed bantering,
when you keep talking into the silence until you
realize my last match has already been spent

and you still have N things to tell me. It's after
another fight has burned down almost to silence,
when you wonder aloud whether we began
with equal amounts each. Whether anything's left.

Aftermath

Why this particular Cleveland pear? What takes
a cherry instead of a plum? Oversized wet flakes

thick in the air, that but for a few degrees would be rain,
settle on still-green leaves, accumulate, strain

branches and trunks. And like people, some break.
In rising wind, a night of cracking. We lie awake.

At dawn, we find splintered limbs littering the lawn,
whole maples down, beeches with their centers gone.

The melt begins, too late. Will birches continue to weep
or lift themselves? Should we cut down or keep

the English oak? Its tendril branches, now unfurled,
no longer hug the trunk; raised arms that swirled

like a figure skater's locked in a spin
hang limp. It may take years for them to fill back in.

Everywhere uprooted shrubs. What to do with a yard
that a Nor'easter has disfigured into a ward

of fresh amputees? Move the debris out of sight
into the woods? It wouldn't make things right,

but we could leave the rest till spring, give the broken
a certain grace. Let this grief remain unspoken.

Anniversary

From the solace of a hot shower beating
on my shoulders and back, through
the misted glass doors out into
the bathroom and beyond
its wall of windows, I discern bands of clouds
peeling from the horizon
heading this way, making alternating strips
of light and shadow that sweep across
the layers of wooded hills
barren of leaves . . .   beyond all that
the interior

           monologue I can't wash away,
the words you gave voice to this morning
about the bands of light and shadow
that constantly sweep across my mind,
always more shadow than light,
the good I do not good enough
to do me enough good, but this time I gave you
time to deliver your monologue
about the help I need to give myself
that would bring the greatest gift
I could give to you.

           Then you left,
and after sitting in the hunt chair
by the window of our bedroom a while,
I left, too,

to take this shower and watch
layer upon layer of shadow
make their uninvited way into the room
and come to me. With my fingers splayed,
I wiped away the mist so I could
see more clearly, feel the waves pass through,
not knowing what else to do.
Everything misted up again, and you—

you passed by the doorway, I thought,
or your shadow did.

Hello, Old Man

"Hello, old man," a voice called out as I
passed by the Kenter Canyon Charter School.
I paused and chuckled. "Hello back," I said
to the girl on the playground swing, knowing
it might be fifty years before she'd understand.
Unrestrained in expressing what they see,
the young are often right. She'd seen white hair.
But for me that day striding up the canyon's
steep hill, four miles into my morning walk,
old age was only a state of mind—
or almost so. Right before the school,
I'd detoured onto a quiet side street
and climbed among some bushes, having spent
the last mile looking for a place to pee.

Remembrance Day, 11/11/11

Uniform and medals in place, he began to recite:
    We few, we happy few, we band of brothers . . .
I let him continue, word for word to the end,
    pausing only for proper punctuation.
Perfect, just as in his prep school days. Blue ribbon.
    Forest of Compiègne, I said. Not Agincourt.
We are the Dead. Short days ago
    We lived, felt dawn, saw sunset glow . . .
He proceeded through the rest of Flanders Fields alone.
    I asked, Can the dead be happy?,

knowing, as I always do, what he'll say:
    Not unless they see sunrise and sunset.
At eleven, the sun was almost as high as it would get.
    They remembered my father
at the chapel, asked how he was doing.
    And as he had the year before, he told them
about his days in flight training, the time
    he flew over his prep school's football field,
almost touching down, almost not making it
    back up, goalposts nearly nicking a wing.

Back then, Henry V was firmly in his place,
    Lieutenant Colonel McCrae too,
but not me, not even an inkling though he knew
    his bride-to-be. Hey, Dad, do you remember
meeting Mum? I asked, and he joked:
    When they heard I'd been given a commission,
they surrendered. So did she, I thought.
    When we came out after the service, we saw

that clouds had gathered on the day,
        the sun strafing them in a few spots.

Over a spot of lunch, we talked about what he could
        remember, pockets of recollection
in odd places and times, his unusual condition unkindly
        rendering some of the unforgettable lost
while leaving much of the forgettable found.
        He recalled the birthday gift for his brother
who guessed what it was after he'd asked and was told
        only that it looked like a hammer.
I asked if he recalled hiking with me, navigations
        by means of compass and map to find

unnamed mountain ponds he could call his own.
        He still did. And also the time he and his brother
set a field of brush ablaze with their father's
        magnifying glass. But not the birth of his son
on the coldest day on record or the party at which
        he met my mother who'd come with
another man. After an early tea, we drove to the lake
        and watched the sky's coals burn down.
He began to recite *Henry V* again.
        It was Saint Crispin's Day. He was king.

At Least One Point

My father always wanted to own an island,
but settled for unnamed ponds
to which he could affix his name for all time.
Armed with compass and large-scale map,
we'd set out in search of those tiny
spots of blue, trying to reach them
before the sun set early in the mountains.
We'd stand at the edge of his discoveries,
linger until there was barely time
to make it back before dark. Hurrying along,
we scrambled through brambles,
slipped on mossy rocks in brooks
as night squeezed out the forest's last light.

One afternoon, frustrated as we kept failing
to find the dot of water the map claimed
was there, losing the battle against
the topography of the place, he thought I might
prefer the challenge of topology instead,
and said, "There is a mountain trail.
You leave the base at eight in the morning
and reach the peak at eight at night,
start back down at eight the next morning,
return to the base at eight that night.
Prove that there is at least one point in time
when you're at the same point on the trail
each day, whether you stop at a stream to drink,
pause to pick newly ripened raspberries,
lie down to contemplate clouds, or not."

My father never settled for clumsy solutions,
some leap of insight always required,
a transformation to an equivalent problem
easy to solve. I couldn't have said,
"Two continuous graphs in the x-y plane,
one for the way up, one for the way down,
must intersect at at least one point."
No—it had to be two people on the same day,
one heading up, the other coming down,
destined to cross paths along the way.

Now that my father is old, I offer
the elegant solution as father and son
meeting somewhere along their journeys—
like my son's ascent and my decline
twenty years hence, he looking up at me
standing at the precipice of dementia
looking down, as I stand now looking up.

New Road

They're busy out on the road, this parade of heavy
equipment. For a week I've watched these guys
while I wait for my son to return from overseas—
a month without news. Every day at 5:30 am,

I've listened to the mammoth grader squeal along
the stripped-down road shearing off stones. Today,
a man leans from a slowly moving truck placing pylons.
Others stand around with coffee and rolls. I ask about

those stakes at regular intervals with Styrofoam plates
stapled to them, signs marked by hand +4, +2, 0, -2, . . .
It's how the road is banked at bends, the foreman says.
They're constantly making adjustments by degrees.

That's what I do, now that my son has graduated
and is looking for work. All preparations finished,
a long narrow truck drops its tarry mix into a machine
that inches along, laying down a one-lane section

of new road, careful to stay aligned with the orange
shoulder markings, steamrollers queued up behind it,
ready to render everything firm and flat, mile after mile.
Not too hard when you already know where it goes.

CRUISING AT SIXTY TO SEVENTY

Not that it's a herd thundering
toward the unseen edge of a precipice—
there are consequences
to plunging over a cliff with hundreds

landing on top of you after your body thuds—
but that's what I'm thinking
as I watch cars on the other side of the Interstate
cruising at sixty to seventy, nobody

realizing that right around the bend
the traffic has come to a dead stop for miles.
They're surfing radio stations, looking for
music they love or news they can tolerate,

or on the phone arguing with their bosses,
engaged in something they're accustomed to.
They likely wouldn't want to be warned,
nothing to do about missed appointments,

few once-in-a-lifetime opportunities
slipping away. Just turned sixty, on my way
to seventy, cruising without a thought
about what lies ahead, I wouldn't want

to be informed either. I haven't yet spent hours
moving nowhere today—I have all the time
I need to get where I'm going, and I'm listening
to a book on CD, *Remarkable Creatures,*

learning about an ichthyosaurus
being chiseled out of a limestone cliff,
imagining myself uncovered, discovered
after millions of years, bones turned to stone.

MAN IN DAY-GLO YELLOW

He'd be a crossing guard
if there were anywhere to cross to,
old man in a reflective vest and standard issue
policeman's hat and light blue shirt

with the flag stitched onto its right sleeve.
He's there in the morning with his
hand-held stop sign to freeze the bustle
when school opens, and in the afternoon

when it lets out. You get the sense
he's an old poet, a certain rhythm
to his motions with the sign
and elegance in his back-and-forth amble

between the corner and the middle of the street.
But mostly it's the furrowed face
and gray ponytail cinched with a band—
you can see him reading to a group

of parents and students, teachers and bus drivers.
Imagine the stories, his thoughts
after a day's work as he walks back
to the apartment complex on the other side

of the tracks. He's the kind you think
it would be interesting to meet and talk to,
but you've never seen anyone do that,
pressed as everyone is to get past each other

when made to come to a full stop and wait,
grumbling under the breath about being
held back like school children, having forgotten
how to suffer the world with grace.

BILLY AND STEPHEN AND ME

for Billy Collins and Stephen Dunn

Billy would tell you about the little flame
at the end of his pen while he rocks in the hammock
listening to wild turkeys rustle last autumn's leaves
as they run toward and away from the stream.

Stephen would tell you he's like the turkeys,
unsure whether he's coming or going,
how that confusion has a certain beauty
which can't be uprooted once it takes hold, and I—

I'm the one in the hammock, reading both
on this first warm day of spring, coming from one
to the other, going back, pausing every few pages
to let the words plant themselves,

and thinking how hard it was last fall
to drill holes in each urn's composite base
so this year's flowers wouldn't drown—
likely red, white, and pink impatiens again,

because habits don't break easily
and those flowers crave shade. Billy would say
there's too much shade in the world,
Stephen that we cast too much on ourselves.

ODE TO LEAVES

Sidewalk strewn after wind and rain,
its cement stenciled with leaves,
stains that will last beyond the next
storm and the next, color-bearing juices
leaching out, last hurrahs as the leaves
exit the world under footsteps and sun
into skeletons of veins that crumble
to dust, a little mulch for next year's

leaves that will look exactly the same—
ovate, cordate, pinnate, spear-shaped,
sword-shaped, rhomboid, lobed—
no generation leaving anything behind,
nothing learned, nothing written down
but buds for next year's crop
to pilfer the sun, do the hard work
of adding pith to core inside the cork.

Their world is pure—never a runoff
for high office, top leaf in town,
no special deals for oak or maple,
nothing under the table, no hanky-panky
in the canopy, just birch to birch,
ash to ash. Simple: leaves like clouds
hanging around, giving shade, sometimes
billowing out, sometimes raining down.

DROUGHT

A long time it has forgotten how to rain,
no grace left, nothing but the old grass roots.
They held on well, but now they must let go,
the well of good intentions run dry.

No grace left, nothing but the old grass roots
on another day the sky is empty,
the well of good intentions run dry
and everyone gone on summer recess.

On another day the sky is empty,
no governor to keep things under control
and everyone gone on summer recess
with temperatures soaring. A system unchecked,

no governor to keep things under control.
Now and then assemblies form
with temperatures soaring. A system unchecked,
and you can hear their thunder

now and then. Assemblies form,
agitate to finally bring some drops of rain,
and you can hear their thunder,
see their underbellies churn charcoal black,

agitate to finally bring some drops of rain.
That threatening yellow-green-purple-gray—
see their underbellies churn charcoal black
clouds that mushroom upward,

that threatening yellow-green-purple-gray
building to a head that might prevail.
Clouds that mushroom upward
refusing to spill, what could you call this?

Building to a head that might prevail,
skies shutting down again, and again
refusing to spill. What could you call this?
This filibuster, how long can it go on,

skies shutting down again and again?
They held on well, but now they must let go
this filibuster. How long can it go on?
A long time. It has forgotten how to rain.

ODE TO A MARTINI

. . . the only American invention
as perfect as the sonnet.
—H.L. Mencken

In training, eight of us, the day before
National Martini Day, already
ruddy from white wine, watch the maestro pour
a splash of Scotch, flavor the rocks, steady
his hand, restrain the ice, drain the pitcher,
then drizzle the gin. We debate how dry
to craft it, how close vermouth's encounter
should be. Just pass the uncapped bottle by,
says one. We settle on a drop apiece,
agree to stir, not shake, drink from the same
giant goblet, make the seeming caprice
a serious toast to friendship, not a game,
no trifling lark, but something well beyond—
we let this crisp concoction build a bond.

FIGURE SKATING

Ever think about how we figure skate
through life? Not so much the hard spills, the cuts
and bruises from which we pick ourselves up,
but those long interludes in the program
meant to set up the key moments—Axels,
Salchows—whether to make them doubles
or triples or the occasional quad.
So much depends on the leaps—the take off,
the time aloft, the sureness of the landing—
that we hardly work on the rest. And when
we have children, it becomes about how well
we prepare them for their big moments,
what we accomplish during the stretch
between their arrival and our departure.
How we hold position in the final spin.

from

LESSONS FROM SUMMER CAMP

2016

New Season

Like a horde of young wizards headed to Hogwarts
(those stories still decades from being written),
we gathered on the platform at Montreal's Windsor Station
in late June, fathers pushing our trunks on trolleys,
mothers fighting back their usual tears, to board the train
for the four-hour voyage into the Laurentian Mountains
and our summer-long stay at camp. The "new boys"
were hesitant, bewildered; the "old boys," together again
after a year apart, smacked each other on the back,
more joyous than they would be at any school reunion.
We were looking forward, not back, the end of summer
infinitely far off. There was little catching up—
talk of school tacitly off-limits—banter about canoe trips
instead, and though we'd never admit it, we, the old boys,
some of us anyway, had become drunk on the camp motto,
not realizing then, not having been told (it would've been
too much like school), that those words we chanted
around the ceremonial fire at Council Ring had been lifted
straight from Thoreau: *Rise free from care before the dawn
and seek adventure. Let the noon find thee by other lakes,
and the night overtake thee everywhere at home.* Some of us
had been homesick all year.

LOST AND FOUND

For good reason the camp made mothers sew
nametags inside their sons' clothing, including socks
and underwear. No need to tell any mother why,
no reason for most Campers to wince at the weekly
lost and found call-out. Directors would hold up
a piece of clothing in the Dining Hall for everyone
to see, then announce the name. How embarrassing
for a boy to keep traipsing up front to claim
his lost apparel, the stack grown high for the serious
offender, the snickers audible. Occasionally,
to make a point, much as they'd do in their positions
at private school, the Directors would hold a boy
for questioning, ask whether he'd ever stopped
to wonder why he had so little to wear. The rest of us
knew these boys would never be named Leaders
if they lasted long enough to become Seniors.
We knew why their parents sent them away.
Still, the camp was too forgiving—no lesson learned
when the lost is always found and then returned,
embarrassment the only consequence of carelessness.

NATURE STUDY

Devil's Paintbrush, pretty orange wildflower
with a yellow center, fiery colors that belie
the softness of the petals, fine brushlike hairs
used by the Devil Himself, seated at a canvas,
to paint Hell. To some "city boys," who spent
their non-summer lives among cement, brick,
steel, tar, and glass, Nature Study was pure hell.
No need for them to learn that white pines
have bundles of five needles and red pines two,
no need to run a hand across smooth or rough
bark to tell what type of tree, or to examine
the shape of a frond to recognize the genus of fern.
For them and many others, the Nature Cabin
was not a favorite place, not even with its
special attractions: de-scented, black-and-white-
striped skunk penned out front and stuffed
loon with all-black head and black-and-white-
spotted back, suspended in full wingspan from
the ceiling inside. But for me, the Nature Cabin
was more than a place to learn the facts of plant
and animal life. Many days, an hour before
the noon gong, armed with my Brownie camera
and a roll of film, I would lie in wait to capture
the Program Director's daughter as she passed by
in short shorts, tank top, and sneakers without
socks, her blond hair in bangs, on her way
to the Dining Hall to fetch her family's lunch.

SNAKE AND FROG

We'd congregated on the beach, none of us
willing to intervene, too intrigued
to see how Nature's predator and prey
would work things out. Most of us
rooted for the frog as it was slowly ingested—
so slowly it seemed as if the snake
doubted itself, that maybe it had realized
its eyes were bigger than its stomach,
better to disgorge the creature before it
became a fat knot stuck in the throat.
Some of us lost interest and continued towards
the Senior Swim Area, content to let our
more bloodthirsty friends reveal the outcome
later, but others remained, a few ophiophilists
(snake-lovers) changing their allegiance
as less and less of the frog showed.
All the while, the frog remained cool, didn't
struggle to escape, exhibited no signs of distress
as the snake "sucked in" one leg and then
the other, working its way bit by bit
up the abdomen until only the frog's head
protruded from the snake's maw. And then—
the reason that one should always stay
to the end—without any warning, when the
snake must have sensed the game was over,
that it had won the contest of wills and was
perhaps a little greedy for results, the snake
opened its jaws wide, and the frog, as if it knew
its time would come, leapt free and kept

leaping, clever enough to stop only
when safely aboard a lily pad in the bay, where there
was time enough to assess the damage,
but not digest the lesson it had just learned.

J-Stroke and Sweep

You can't see the metaphor when you're a Camper
or Counselor. You're not looking for it.
A canoe is just a canoe, a paddle just a paddle.
At camp, you learn the J-stroke to keep your canoe
on course. You practice it, intrigued that a straight
stroke modified at its end with a flourish, the lower
hand on the paddle turning out and away from the canoe
to form a letter J (or its mirror image), allows you
to maintain course. Later in life, you see people
out on rivers and lakes who think that paddling
first on one side, then the other, back and forth,
is the proper way to keep a canoe headed straight.
Sometimes you see them sitting in the stern,
their weight too far back, the bow out of the water.
Better to sit in the bow seat facing backwards,
you'd like to tell them. You know. But the canoe is
wider there, and they'd have to shift from side to side
to paddle alternately on the left and right. At camp,
you learned to kneel in the center, straddling
the portage thwart, one leg over it and one up against it
from behind, as if you were praying to the god of wind.
And if that god's wind is heavier than a breeze, and if
you're traveling broadside to the waves—because that
is your intended course—you soon learn it's a different
stroke you require. You must paddle on the leeward side
with a broad, sweeping motion that pushes the bow
back into the wind. At camp, the J-stroke and sweep
work well. It's only later you discover their limitations.
As a Counselor, you had experience with children,

other people's, not yours—you had them in your care
only for the summer. Less commitment, the stakes
not as high. But with your own, there's seldom anything
as simple as J-stroke and sweep to keep matters
in balance. And in marriage, too, the winds shift
constantly. No technique or tool or amount of practice
seems adequate, and often it's not as much a question
of staying the course as finding where you need to go.

Night Overtake Thee

Everywhere is home—something you might hear
a Buddhist say. At peace with the world
around you, easier, you've found, on a canoe trip
than back home. You pass through lakes
and pause, as water drips from the end
of your paddle resting across the gunwales,
to take in what you can't see but only feel.
If noon finds you by other lakes,
so will night, a new place or an old one
revisited. You cook a meal over an open fire,
eat a wild-blueberry pie you baked in
a reflector oven, its crust rolled thin on the hull
of your canoe with a tin can. You launch
a lifetime love of cooking. You pitch your tent
under pines, listen to them talk in the wind.
They try to tell you something
you won't hear until many years later.
Most nights you find clarity in the darkness
of the wilderness, let your mind run free.
More stars than you ever expected to see.
Up there, alien places where you can imagine
beings by other lakes, loons calling to them too.
Tonight, you find yourself at home in the forest
of another galaxy. Tomorrow, morning mist
will rise and you'll watch a doe drink cautiously
on the far side, sensing she is not alone.
You'll discover a lake that is clear to the bottom,
fill your pannikin to quench your thirst.

Swimming Lessons

Many of us already knew how to swim well by the time
we first arrived at camp, having been taught
by our mothers or fathers during picnics at lakes.
We knew how to swim freestyle or "crawl" as it was
called back then. Or thought we did. We knew
we hadn't yet grasped the proper technique
for other strokes. Sidestroke was so easy it hardly
needed to be taught, but breaststroke and backstroke—
they were harder. The head swimming instructor,
Mr. Titus, was relentlessly demanding—he'd stand
atop the tower at the Senior Swim Area to take
a bird's-eye view of our every flaw, the left leg
in the "whip kick" not sweeping its arc symmetrically
with the right, a foot flexed when it should be
pointed, the head submerged too far in this stroke
or that, the kick always too vigorous, fingers splayed
wide apart when they should have been held together
loosely. "You don't have webbed hands," he'd say.
His surname spoke to a certain Romanesque strength,
and watching him pull himself through the water
seemingly with arms alone, only the upper half
of his body visible, an occasional flutter from his feet
piercing the surface, we couldn't help but wonder if he
were merely half a man, nothing below the waist.
Breathing alternately to the left and right, his mouth
opened into a perfect letter O, each exhale a barely
audible cleansing breath, he propelled his torso
with slow, steady strokes, lap after lap for an hour.
Mesmerizing, monotonous. When he finally emerged

from the water, utterly relaxed as if he'd just stepped
out of a steaming shower, we were sure he wasn't
entirely human. We knew we could never be like him.
Still, when we became Counselors, he trusted us
to teach the young boys, supporting them under their
backs or stomachs to let them get the sense of floating,
then kneeling beside them in shallow water, our faces
submerged, showing them how to breathe more and more
slowly, until it seemed they were hardly breathing at all.

Running Free

Campers would rather trim sails than hear about
close hauled and broad reach,
clew and luff, halyards and sheets,
the rules of racing and right-of-way.
Bow and stern, port and starboard, they could abide,
but they wanted to get their hands on a rope,
their feet under hiking straps. Wanted to
sail in a stiff breeze so the boat could heel.
Couldn't wait for the day when they graduated
to skip and took the tiller. All were eager to race
before they'd learned to bring the boat safely
into dock and secure it in a finger, yet too few
learned that winning a race often means
sailing well on the upwind leg where the boats
are at their slowest and it's all about being the best
close hauled—that was "boring," they said;
they wanted to run free.

Lights Out

It was no challenge back then to quiet my mind
after the palaver in the dark suddenly stilled
to sporadic words, then nothing . . .
Sheer exhaustion was enough, and if not,
the humming of crickets, wind in the leaves,
the splashing of waves . . . Much easier back then
when those were real and close at hand,
harder now when merely remembered,
harder to let go, extinguish the excitements
and disappointments now that I carry mine
and my children's, my wife's . . .
It's always a night in the wilderness, but there's
no popping of a fire's dying embers
to distract me; it's no longer as simple as
killing the last pesky mosquito whining
in my ear. There's no Officer of the Day
to call Lights Out!, nobody but me
to shut down the background chatter in my brain,
lower the wick and snuff out the lantern,
my wife having long since gone to sleep.

Houses of Parliament

How long they'd been called that, Lower House,
primarily for the Juniors, and Upper House
for the Intermediate and Senior Campers,
we never found out, but long before our time,
the foul smell emanating from them
must have inspired the eminent names.
The Counselors had to use them, too, no place
of greater refinement available to the bosses
of our summer lives. Out beyond the tent line,
out there in the valley on the way back from
the Dining Hall, the Houses were outhouses
in every sense. Quiet places in the woods
for time out from the daily routine—
after breakfast, to contemplate the coming
events; after lunch, an interlude to start
to digest what you'd just taken in and expel
what you'd hadn't yet absorbed; in the evening,
right before bed, as darkness began to
blanket everything except the thin lines
of the birches, a moment to get beyond
the biting of the insistent mosquitoes attracted
by the pervasive stink and pass a new piece
of legislation. Our friends from below the
border didn't mind the imposition of a different
form of democracy, though one day, courtesy
of their overnight efforts, we awakened to new
signs on our places of congress—same two
chambers, same stalls, same wicked stench,
but now marked *House of Representatives*
and *Senate*. All the toilet paper was gone.

Letters

Once a week, during the Rest Hour after lunch,
all Campers were forced to write a letter.
Most any letter was considered good enough,
usually one sent off to parents for the younger boys,
possibly to a girlfriend for the older boys,
and after the first ten days of camp, every Counselor
was required to write a letter to the parents
of each boy under his care in his tent, a note
that invariably glossed over what wasn't working,
and fabricated, as necessary, things that were— .
a cheery, upbeat account of the thrills
their son was experiencing for the first time at camp,
or again, as he had last year. Fill in the blanks.
Imagine my parents' surprise when they
compared a letter they'd received from my brother
with the one from his Counselor. Everyone
had thought that my brother, seven years younger,
was destined to have the same gleeful
experience as I had as a Camper. His letter
featured a stick-figure sketch of his Counselor,
which he labeled R.F. How sweet, my parents thought.
The letter was typical of a Camper's note home—
short, conveying little that was illuminating,
apart from, in my brother's situation,
his dislike of the nine-hole golf course with its
too-short holes and its dirt "greens."
R.F.'s letter mentioned that my brother had been
found one night, by a Counselor patrolling
after Lights Out, with his feet protruding from

his sleeping bag. My brother had worked his way in
head-first, his way, we learned later,
of muffling his sobs. Rat Fink had been right—
my brother wasn't having a good time.
They'd assumed he was another me. He wasn't.

Visitors' Day

Picnic Beach raked clean, extra tables scattered about,
Counselors on duty along the road into camp
to direct parents to park in the Campcraft Area—
Visitors' Day, a day I could never figure out
whether parents looked forward to
more than their sons, an opportunity to gauge that all
was well, a gamble of sorts, because if all was not—
well, there was little that could be done,
homesick Campers seldom allowed by their parents
to leave prematurely after all those non-refundable fees
had already been paid. How I felt
changed during the course of the day, anticipation
at the start, waiting for my parents' car to crest the hill,
hoping they wouldn't be the last to arrive.
It was a chance to show off what I'd learned
during the first few weeks, and, I suppose, an affirmation
that I was missed. (They always put on a good show.)
One year, my grandparents came along
and brought a picnic. We spent the morning at the beach
and swam under the watchful eye of a lifeguard,
no need to pair up with a buddy that day,
no random whistles to check that everyone was present
and accounted for, a little freedom
from the normal routine. I remember showing my parents
my improved proficiency with an axe,
chopping a poplar log into sections, then splitting those
for firewood, saying I wanted an axe of my own
back home. "But we have no trees," my father said

too quickly. "At least none I want cut down."
By the end of Visitors' Day, I was ready for all guests
to leave, certain that enough politeness had been served up,
the invasion having lasted too long, the call of friends
once again overpowering the call of family.
But when my parents' car disappeared around the bend,
I'd always, even as a Senior Camper, find myself
wiping tears from my cheeks, as I do now
when my grown sons leave after a visit home.

NEW POEMS

It's Time to Talk

with a nod to Lewis Carroll

I like oysters, not stuffed and baked the way the carpenter
might have preferred, but raw, on the half-shell, especially

after all the work to pry them open. I don't know about
my friend, the walrus, who's been trying hard to avoid being

devoured by a shark. When he graces me with his company
along the oceanfront, I skip stones as we talk of many things.

Today, it was not about the odd family standing knee-deep
having a photo taken for posterity, the sea not boiling hot

in late autumn, nor whether pigs have wings, which they do,
of course, at the Flying Pig Restaurant with its scrumptious

barbecue-pork pizza. We talked not of cabbages, but kings,
the kind who'd tell you that you can no longer skip stones.

Outdoor Fire

Trying to suss out whether absence is enemy
or friend, we sit side by side in Adirondack
chairs, our minds in the flames licking up
the chimney's inner brick face, a fire we started
in the right place for once. *It's okay to get*

tired of hearing yourself think, she says,
so long as you don't feel that I need to know.
But what if I want to know what you think,
I ask, *and you just sit there glazed over,*
the fire having turned your face to glass?

Then look at me and see yourself, she says.
And that's why I make a fire every night, I say,
to see myself in your eyes. Hour by hour
I keep it stoked. Sparks burst through
the chimney cap's fine mesh, shower down

around us. The birds have settled for the night,
the tree frogs silent too. It's only male crickets
who chirp, I've learned—females do not
speak their piece. *Listen,* she says—*like you,*
they are still going strong. I am not.

Return to Oia

I have returned to Villa Katikies overlooking
Santorini's gaping maw. To a view of the site
of a cataclysm thousands of years ago.
In predawn's diffuse light, I lie in the hot tub
outside my room, trying to imagine
the devastation. Its mortar cracking, Atlantis
shook. Block by block, buildings crumbled,
tumbled into a mounting pile of rocks.
The shoreline cinched like a hangman's knot,
squeezed out a breathless people's last gasps,
the great civilization rent, fed to a sea
that could not be satisfied. With a giant,
final slurping suck, it swallowed the city whole,
then belched an aftershock outward
through the isles, the expanding waves
an SOS in a not-yet-invented Morse Code,
peaks and troughs carrying a story of screams
silenced into nothingness. The volcano
thundered through the night, launched geysers
of stone and ash skyward.

With intermittent blasts,
cruise ships pronounce their progress
toward the port. Roused birds ride the air
on extended wings, greet another day with song
that will be lost when the village stirs.
I swish my arms, send ripples that reflect
off the tiled walls, an SOS of my own:
I have returned to Oia alone.

And Still the Earth Is Shaking

—arrange the numbers 1 to 4, each
occurring twice, so that between
the appearances of the number n,
there are n numbers.

Took longer than it should have, but I figured
it out, the correct string of numbers, not a
combination to a lock I had forgotten, nor a
key to understanding the incomprehensible,
but the solution to a puzzle my mind had been
turning over since the latest horrific news
for the planet, the death of more than 50,000
this time. Reminds me of when Richter 7.8
struck China and buried 900 schoolchildren.
Now, the same for these new victims and their
survivors, who'll try to carry on in the world
when they'll only want to be anywhere else,
so long as it's with their lost ones, even in
an alternate universe where the unthinkable
didn't take place because fault lines don't
exist there and slippage can't occur, a place
assembled according to a different set of rules,
a kinder geology, yet where beauty can still
be found. So, yes, I have solved that number
puzzle, but can't fathom these too-large
numbers, can't imagine a man holding the
hand of his deceased 15-year-old daughter
still pinned under the rubble of their home,
or two breathless brothers locked in a final

embrace. Instead, once again, I must distance
myself from a tragedy. Play some music,
read a book, go for a walk, forever unable to
figure out why any god would let this happen.

Unable to See Our Way Clear

A nearly symmetric tree, spilling
its leaves like a fountain
by the pool, the weeping cherry
appears the same from all angles
in daytime, left side indistinguishable
from the right, but not at night, one half
yellowish, ground-lit by incandescent
bulb, the other bright white, an LED,
the contrast then as stark as in
the aftermath of the latest deaths
by gunfire, when we find ourselves
once again split in two, unable to see
our way clear to turning off the lights
and waiting for the sun to rise.

Milkweed and Beech

The milkweed hung on this year, late seeds
in fluff, stuffed in pods shut tight. The beech,
as usual, held most of its leaves. Burnished
to bronze, then dulled to brown, enough surrendered
to lay bare what summer's green had masked—
a nest built by hornets slathering
their saliva over fibers gathered
from the hillside patch of milkweed, making
layers of gray paper to encase
their hive. When at last it came to light,
how could anyone not see what had been
there always, those creatures high in the tree
conspiring out of sight who knows how long,
milkwood and beech, standing back, standing by?

A Forest of Begonias

Every year, I plant begonias in the front
and back yards, and around the bases of trees,
lush gardens of them. Not perennials, they
remain in flower until the first frost, when

overnight, the fleshy stalks, so sturdy during
the onslaught of summer, freeze and wilt.
Until the year that autumn doesn't arrive,
Earth not tilting any differently on its axis,

but everything else instead that led to reaching
the point of no return. The begonias grow
taller, become trees. Year after year, they
continue to gain stature, their once knobby

and gangly stems thicken, turn into smooth
hardwood. No longer delicate, they crowd out
and stunt other growth, assert themselves
over those at whose feet they used to kneel,

a new order in the forest. Never any of their
blossoms covering the floor, no more a good
reason to shed the only thing that long ago they
might have called beautiful about themselves.

When a Hydrant Is Blue

After I'd noticed a spectrum of colors
used for hydrants around town, I might
have guessed that the painters had

chosen palettes to express their moods.
Turns out black merely signifies
a hydrant retired from further use,

and blue promises maximum water flow
when it's tapped—too much that
is combustible lying nearby.

Now something new has been added
to the old code, a yellow band wrapped
below the blue bonnet, hydrant after

hydrant along a street, perhaps the first
placed by a refugee displaced during
the war that is not a war, a sign

of her prayers for family left behind,
then sympathizers following suit,
a plea to stop setting the world on fire.

CHILD COLORING IN A WAR ZONE

Sitting on the stone steps of her broken home,
mother and father already gone,
only her grandmother left, the girl colors
the jigsaw of the girl in her coloring book,
who's sitting on the steps of her own broken home
on an empty street. She likes that each piece
is a number because she's always liked numbers.
She fills in the 1 with sky-blue, then 2 and 3
with leaf-green, wonders what to do
with the number she doesn't recognize, an 8
fallen on its side. Looking at the plus sign,
she imagines the crosshairs of a sniper
turning her into a minus. Out of crayons and hope,
she, too, will become a number in a war
she's been told is not a war. At another 8,
right-side up, her age, she stops, at last
understanding the number 0 she left blank,
her alone in a world no longer here, the shadow
seeping down the page blood-red.

Acorns Falling on Our Heads

This would be good news if you were a squirrel
and the work of shaking them loose

were kindly being done on your behalf.
But you're more like Chicken Little,

who's frantic over those fallen bits of sky,
the world around you tumbling down.

And yet, you want those acorns to keep falling
for the little good they might do if they land

on enough heads, knocking some sense
into those who keep sowing their bad seeds.

Gardening

Mild winter, acorns not buried under snow,
no need for squirrels to access the cache
they'd stored underground in random spots,
and so, come spring, oak shoots popped up
all over her garden. She started plucking
those poking through the creeping phlox
in full pink and violet bloom hanging over
the wall along the driveway. Hard work,
the new growth having burst through
their seed shells, the husks refusing to cede
easily to her tugs. She should have caught
them earlier. Yet, she was able to render
the effort near-effortless by attaching names
to the weeds she ripped out by the roots:
Mr. Speaker of the House and Mr. Senate
Minority Leader; Your Honorable Associate
Justice; then sweeping through the lesser
lights she judged to be too much in their
element, but actually out of place, not in it
for the common good. She extracted one after
another until she'd amassed a considerable
pile of would-be-righteous oaks that, when
they grew up, would have thought themselves
upright citizens in the community. All this
without using toxic chemicals. If only.

STALKING PREY

In a poem years ago, my beagle puppy,
Sadie, leads me to a field where we
have trespassed many times. I marvel
at how well she tracks, sniffing and snuffling,
snout pressed to the ground, towards

a rabbit hole, or deer romping through
the woods, or fox dissolving into a thicket,
a hunter stalking her quarry, driven by
instincts lodged deep in her lupine past.
But now, we have aged into another poem,

our roles exchanged. Older and wiser,
we stay indoors. Today, she lies curled
against my feet amidst a stack of day-old
newspapers. I have moved on. Scrolling
through my laptop screen, I chase the telltale

print further into the X-President's swamp,
but he is elusive as ever. Sometimes,
I come so close I allow myself to believe
that we will finally hunt him down, and I can
see that Sadie is also lost in a dream.

GOATLAND

The thing that particularly stands out
about the recently completed U.S. census
of goats is their extreme concentration
in the State of Texas. Not that there
aren't more, best seen by piling 500
of the animals into a single light grey dot
on the map, darkened spots then appearing
in California, Arkansas, Illinois, and a few
others, but there is a large area of Texas
that is black, no doubt reflecting Texans'
changing habits regarding the mohair
they wear, the meat they eat, the milk
they drink, and the cheese they make.
Not to speak of the grass and brush they
need to keep trimmed. In one place alone,
goats outnumber people 22:1. Presumably,
polls will soon be taken to add goats to
the voter rolls, the state having become
too blue for some goatherders' tastes.
Goats are making their mark on the local
culture. Imagine a proposal to fit special
seats for the wooly creatures in theaters.
And that video game, Goat Simulator,
with goats yelling like humans, a mere
reflection of humans yelling like goats
in the halls of government these days.

The Two Owls

For warding off the unwelcome, I have relied
on my old sentry, a crested owl mounted

on a pole on my backyard deck
like a scarecrow, her primary target

a relentless downy woodpecker tacka-tacka-
tacking new holes beneath the eaves.

I am the other owl, scanning for breaking news
of the tacka-tacka-tacking going on in the world.

Stopping by Woods

On a morning with no breeze in the trees, only a few
clouds on high, and my mind as clear as the sky,
my walk along the stretch of bike trail near White Pond
was as unremarkable as it had ever been until
the stillness was abruptly broken by a flicker flapping
its wings in distress against the bark of a pine.

It was camouflaged so well I could have passed by
without seeing those magnificent yellow tailfeathers,
the wings spread full as the bird tried to extricate
its vine-snared claw, nature having trouble sorting
itself out that day. I didn't venture into the woods
to try my hand at what the flicker failed to achieve.

Whether I possessed the free will to decide the matter
on my own or was just subconsciously impelled to
intervene, I couldn't leave well enough alone. For this
creature trapped by circumstance, it would turn out to be
a lucky day—I called the Harwich Conservation Trust
and they sent someone out to cut her free.

THE TOWN IN ITS WISDOM CUTS OUR TREES

Long markers along the edges of roads,
they're disappearing. Men clad in dayglo vests
atop their towering nests take limb after limb
with chainsaws. Trees marked by red ribbons
will soon be stumps—a pandemic
cutting down the borer-infested ash
and anything judged past its prime, leaving
mostly the young and healthy not yet grown
tall enough to tear down power lines
when rains loosen their parents' root balls
and winds wrestle the crowns to the ground.

I stand guard over one of my favorites,
an old sweetgum still sound, daring the workers
grinding into dust a hundred years of history
stored in cordwood born when there was
just a farmhouse near and a few barns,
little of the original pastureland remaining now,
three cows slouching in the grass. I'm at
the stone wall where a pack of alpacas
have gathered, the largest of the lot
with light shaggy fur facing me as if she wants
to talk, as if she thinks I will have an answer.

Someone's God Somewhere

Cordoned off yards above the high-tide line,
      Pleasant Beach has had no visitors for weeks
while a cutter suction dredger anchored
      in the inlet to Cockle Cove goes about its work—

the boat's powerful pump sucks sand
      from the channel bottom and transports it
through a wide-mouth pipe sunk under
      the surface of Nantucket Sound and snaked

two-thirds of a mile along the shore to rise
      like a gigantic sea worm onto the empty beach
to restore the coastline, subdue an increase
      in the no longer random erosion that weather

brings more often now, a minor victory
      for the town against the onslaught of nature
at the expense of satiating the cutter's thirst
      for fossil fuel, another war that can't be won

in the end, only a momentary addition of extra
      space for beachgoers to root themselves in chairs
out of the sun under umbrellas, escaping
      their lives napping or reading books that likely

have just collected dust on nightstands,
      attention spans cut short these days like the lives
of beaches washed out to sea, farmlands
      baked dry from lack of rain while oceans rise,

waterways flood, forests disappear, wildlife loses
    its natural habitat, the order of things
disturbed by someone's god somewhere on a rampage,
    not by us merely going about our lives.

Unsung Hymn During the Time of Covid

They shut the doors at Our Lady of Grace—
it's closed for the season, as if come fall
no need to soothe one's soul in a holy place.

In the parking lot, there's finally space—
you'd think they'd be saying, "Come one, come all!"
but the doors are shut at Our Lady of Grace.

In this time of Covid, why not embrace
the chance to welcome us back? It's no small
need to soothe one's soul in a holy place.

No one-way road to redemption, no race
to be first to speak out, utter the call,
"Unshutter the doors at Our Lady of Grace."

They will not repent this serious disgrace,
the chapel locked up, no priest standing tall
with a need to soothe souls in a holy place.

Without doubt our trust was sadly misplaced.
We vowed to wear masks throughout it all.
Still, they shut the doors at Our Lady of Grace,
refused to soothe souls in her holy place.

Gale-Force Winds

The breeze off the western reservoir
riffles the air in the gaps
between the backyard deck's floorboards.
Its song starts as flute-like whines.

Those soft moans become groans,
a bassoon's longer-lived grumbling roar
building to a rage more outspoken
and violent, too few leaves left to impede

the mounting blow. The gale passes through
almost-bare branches and slams against
the house. Drafts sift in around the windows;
my wife wraps her comforter close.

We turned the clocks back last Sunday,
but only an hour. Our friends remind us
that we can't turn farther back,
not even a few years, for another run

at how things ought to be. With too little
cover afforded by my anorak,
I hold onto the railing and peer out over
layers of graying hills. It won't be long now.

FRAYING

Almost a constant out here on Cape Cod,
the winds blow hard, sometimes gale force,

like those that storm through life these days.
And lots of flagpoles with large flags,

many oversized for their masts. They seldom
lie limp, often flap wildly, shouting out

their stars and stripes, but inevitably, they
tatter in the wind and then fray further until

the free end resembles a ragged coastline.
Month after month, they stay unattended,

seemingly little interest in replacing them,
as if there is no longer enough cash on hand

for making everything great again, a sign
of what is, rather than what is yet to come.

Cairn

Against sea and sky, the cairn looks like the head
and body of a statue. It has stood for years,
a tower of four stones balanced on a groin,
withstanding heavy winds and crashing waves.
Time has made it more secure, smaller
and smaller stones wedged in the spaces
between the larger, a solemn testimonial
built by several perennial walkers along this
strip of beach, likely none having met any
of the others. But now, vandals have done
what the weather could not, destruction
the easier path in this ongoing battle
of rebuilding, leveling, rebuilding, both sides
committed to their cause, unwilling to relent.

SAFE HARBOR

Buried deep in the Sound, a tetrapod of poles
supporting a crow's nest with two "red, right,
returning" triangular signs, a beacon

for boats coming back to a harbor sheltered
from rough seas. Out here on the long jetty
with flat-topped boulders forming a wide

walkway, you know that the winds won't blow
you away; you'll be okay holding onto your hat
and stepping past the bits of crab shells

and claws left by gulls. You've come out today
because the skies are finally clear, and, for
a few moments, you can get far enough away.

The Bell

On a path in the woods, I met an off-leash dog sporting a large cow bell, the dog's matted fur hanging like rags. Around a bend in the trail, I met the dog's gaunt master wearing a mud-streaked windbreaker with a ripped sleeve, his tangled gray hair hanging in thick strings to his shoulders, his bulbous, veined nose as prominent as the dog's snout. Both dog and man appeared somewhat lost. I wondered why the man wasn't wearing a bell too. He looked unkempt, unfed, homeless. Penniless, I thought. Maybe I should buy him a dinner and the dog some food, take them both to a shelter for the night. Yet, I kept on going. Sometimes, a person, even a dog, doesn't know where to go, but merely goes anyway. Sometimes, the thoughts that tag along take a turn. A year later, I met the same man, same dog, on the same trail, and this time, I joined them. We walked together out of the woods, talking over that clanging bell, this time in the winter's cold, the dog clad in somewhat less-filthy fur, the man in an orange toque and navy coat hanging down below his knees. Back on the bike path, I watched them mount a low sandy ridge, descend to a paved street, then enter the driveway of a one-story Cape-style home. He opened the front door.

Sharing the Trail

One can't help but wonder if it actually
happened, a journey one day along
the Old Cape Rail Trail, commenced on wheels,
terminated on foot, someone tired of
riding who found a spot off-trail to park
her bike and then walk home, someone else
inspired by Duchamp's ready-made bicycle
wheel implanted in a four-legged stool
desiring to fashion a copycat
piece of eco-art—her entire bicycle
piercing an oak tree—his not-so-subtle
warning to walkers and bikers alike
to share the trail, calling out "on your left"
or "on your right" before passing by.

WHY I PREFER NUMBERS TO WORDS

Their appeal lies in their lack of emotion,
in their even keel, even when they yield an odd
outcome, better yet when they're whole, not

fractional or irrational, when positive, not
negative. Notwithstanding the irony of harnessing
words to extol the primacy of numbers, they

surpass words in their raceless, genderless existence
without religion. They seldom cause wars.
They wear a universal identity, all people's

numbers our numbers, anyone's mathematical
exploits the world's to savor. It's a marvel
how hard it can be to prove a simple statement

like Fermat's last theorem, the years that those
who love numbers will strive to leave their mark,
devote to prise out an elegant result, declare:

I, too, have lived and made a difference!
To stake a claim to fame that will stand beyond
the time when people yet to come have gone.

Poet and Mathematician

Let's go for a walk while there is still
time in the autumn of this country.
It is past bright colors into the drab
browns that precede the winter's snows.

Show me the way to a place where
none of this makes sense.

Listen—the only birds around are crows.
Their voices are shrill.
We must go.

We'll get lost.

No more than we are now, my friend.
There are no easy flights.
Unlike the crows, we don't have wings.

I'm seeing a decision tree that branches,
and you're saying go this way
without knowing where we'll get to.

You're the mathematician—
you know all paths through the forest
converge at infinity.

You're the artist—you must mean
a vanishing point where we don't exist
though we carry the past with us.

Wherever we end up, we will bring those
grains of sand filling our shoes.

THE GRAPH OF YOU

I've been thinking of you,
and I've been thinking about
graphs, those mathematical
objects composed of lines
joining one point to the next.

With a finger, I draw a line
from A to B along your body,
knowing where that will lead—
my flesh touching your flesh,
healing each other's wounds.

Transfixed in a Waltz

You see metal forests; I see new farms
enhancing the old ones, manmade structures
capturing sunmade currents of wind that
sweep across the land. You see whirling blades
chopping wings off birds in flight. To me, they're
petals on giant white stalks, arms that swirl
with grace, a dance against the sky. To you,
glinting knives—unnatural, unwanted,
even if necessary in these times.
Instead, why don't I be one tower, you
another, I mesmerized by your moves,
our lines perfectly synchronous, your arc
matching the curve of mine, us locked as one,
momentarily transfixed in a waltz?

You Choose to Die in Your Bed

in memory of my sister-in-law, 1965–2016

The doctors honored your request to stay
at home in your own bed. You chose
the side you've always slept on, near
the window through which, when you are
conscious for moments that no longer
linger, you can watch the remaining leaves—
everything else just branches and twigs—
detach in the wind. Now you hear wings,
the birds also on their way. It's the passing
of fall, this final falling away, leaf by leaf,
bird by bird, and you, pound by pound,
your body nearly weightless now, skin
drawn tight over bones almost porous,
you light enough to be able, at last, to fly.

Handing Down

for my son Jack

The target market must have been rather small—
not many coffee drinkers want to start the day
holding a ceramic cup that makes all those
high school word problems in math look trivial
compared to the scribblings in thin white lines

on the exterior of that unusual gray-green mug,
not merely algebra and geometry, but calculus,
too, with its differentiations and integrations.
I've been trying to figure out in whose younger
hands I can place this precious object before

I'm gone, someone to appreciate what's on
the outside as well as the inside, to start the day
with a fresh brew and a mind open to possibilities,
but I'm stuck thinking about that quadratic
formula $x^2 + y^2 = z^2$ with its companion sketch

of a double cone, reminding me of something
tastier—a vanilla soft-swirl ice cream at the local
Dairy Queen—and the challenge I could never
master: no matter how fast I licked it, calculating
how long before it melted all over my hands.

Ode to a Golfer

for my son Brad

A Passel of Sticks

A young boy clutching a passel of sticks,
cap slightly askew, clad against the autumn
chill in a blue sweater with a row of white
flags across the chest, out-of-focus yellow
maple leaves visible in the background,
a young boy, my boy, at age two about to
run away from home, but caught in the act . . .
the look on your face one of surprise at being
found out, mouth open to say: *You can't
stop me!* What were the sticks for, I wanted
to ask, thinking you might have in mind
building a house in the woods, a place of
your own, where mommy and daddy couldn't
tell you what to do, not do.

Irons and Woods

When you were four, I took you to the golf
course with irons and woods, your new sticks.
You spent hours in greenside *sand pots*
learning how to make bunker shots that
came to rest near the cup, the up and down
of life beginning to play out as you rose
through the ranks as a junior, competed in
national championships, led your college
team, then tried your hand for years as a pro,
becoming an amateur again when that
didn't pan out. You won for the U.S. against
France and Ireland, brought home trophy
after trophy, and finally, at age thirty-nine,
were named regional Player of the Year.

BARE BRANCHES

We sit by a bonfire that was hard to start
in the freezing weather, feed it twigs,
small branches, and several large ones we've
sawed into sections, all blown to the ground
and scattered about by the recent
once-in-a-generation winter storm.
A hawk, red-tailed perhaps, perches high
on a thin branch in an oak across the road,
the lens of my cellphone's camera not
strong enough at full zoom to distinguish
one kind from another. In the opposite
direction, where the sun has set, a narrow
crescent moon hides behind a tangle
of branches, silhouettes against the sky.

Bundled against the cold, my two grown sons
and I celebrate Christmas Day together,
recall incidents from their childhood
they found humorous, often at my expense.
My two granddaughters have chosen to stay
indoors, likely content to be with their
mother reading books, or merely absorbed
playing by themselves, young minds forgetting
the fun they have helping their father
build a fire. I wonder why he hasn't
insisted they join us, missing a chance
for one last three-generation moment
at the home he plans to sell and move on,
something to remember after I'm gone.

On The Merits of Taking Up Pickleball

On a walk through any community park
with racquetball sports, if it's still morning,
you can't miss it, the pickleball courts
all taken by seniors getting their daily
exercise. I often stop and watch,
applauding the skill these older folk
display. They're a competitive lot,
the ladies especially. This morning I saw
a pretty woman with a red ponytail
grin as she smashed a high ball away
for a point. My wife tells me I should take up
the game, too much time on my hands,
she says, it would be a good way for you
to meet new people. I would need a lot
of practice first, I say—it's been thirty years
since I've played tennis, and I stopped
because my ex-wife finally beat me
when I developed what might now recur
as chronic pickleball elbow. But you claim
they're ancient, she counters, and you
aren't quite there yet. Aren't you concerned
that I'll latch onto a sexy single woman
to teach me to play, I ask. We might be
so good together she'd want me as her
permanent partner. Don't get carried away,
she says. You're not *that* young.

Painting

He kept up his long walks by the river
into autumn, wild asters on the bank
thriving in the cold, nearby tall spikes
of hollyhocks well past, except a few
lingering blooms. The milkweed hung on
stubbornly, refused to yield their seeds.
Years ago, he and his mother would
gather stalks after the pods had opened
and the fluff had blown away. He painted
the pods' insides mostly silver or gold,
sometimes poppy red, her favorite fall
color, arranged the dried plants in vases
for sale at the church bazaar. Years ago.
He still paints them. Now, nothing but red.

He Could Still See the Light

in memory of my father, 1925–2015

My father, the physics professor, well understood
electricity and magnetism, knew that their fields,
oscillating at right angles to each other, constituted

waves of light, taught his students that Maxwell's
equations, expressed in the calculus of divergence
and curl, governed their evolution, but his affection

for the sun's rays came only late in life following
several heart attacks, when his heart thrummed
at a minuscule measure of its once-vigorous force,

his blood barely reaching his fingers and toes,
poor man forever cold. He could still see the light,
yet ended his days constantly seeking its warmth.

CHANNELING PLATO

It's been nearly eight years since I last wrote
to you, father, yet here I sit at the antique
walnut desk with letter paper set out
on the inlaid leather top. I remember
drawing points and lines, making planar
graphs to disprove your latest conjecture
about how to demonstrate elegantly
the truth of the famous coloring theorem.

I pick up the brass icosahedral paperweight
and turn it in my hand, the key, I have
hypothesized, to the theorem—it never failed
a test I subjected it to, but in the end, fell
short of a watertight proof. How strange
the Greeks with their four elements and five
regular polyhedra. How ironic that Plato
chose to assign the icosahedron to water.

But now, as I write, I imagine the shape
of fire instead, the flame you kindled
in my brain by way of math conundrums
you posed on our walks. Plato again,
the tetrahedron, its four apexes like licking
flames, fire struck into being by matchsticks,
six assembled into four triangular faces,
the very first puzzle you gave me to solve.

I can't recall anything based on the earthly
cube or airy octahedron. Dodecahedron—
the fifth Platonic solid—is not an element
at all. To you, it stood for something like
the quintessence of thought. As I placed your
ashes into the ground, I found it hard to breathe,
not inspiring air in that moment, but thinking
of the love for math you handed down.

WHITEFACE MOUNTAIN

Whiteface Mountain beckons again, its snow-covered trails not yet caught in the rising sun. I'm here in retreat from a world more clearly cruel to recall how much I loved skiing until, with my son on a mogul field, I caught a tip, tumbled down the slope and came to rest in a heap. My right calf stabbing, I finished the run on only one ski. And haven't skied since, but imagine myself on unbroken snow, carving narrow S-turns down the fall line in the cold.

I remember a day here with my father long ago when we could not bundle ourselves enough to stay warm, the ponchos they handed us for the long ride in the chairlift doing little good against the wind. It took the fire in the summit lodge to thaw us out before we could head back down, only to turn around, ride up again, and sit by the fire, as I do now at the base lodge. My son, waiting for the lifts to open, hands me the morning paper with all the news.

White Pond

When breaking news envelops me in its
straitjacket and I have to wriggle free,
a visit to this freshwater kettle pond helps
settle my mind. If nobody else is here,

I sit on the overturned skiff tied to an old
oak that shades me in summer, showers me
with acorns in the fall. Sometimes
a raft of brown ducks swims by, once

a pair of white swans. But it's the seagulls
who favor the pond as much as I do,
joining me no matter the season. They circle
in narrowing spirals, then alight gently,

whether the pond is calm or rough.
They gather on the far side, each gliding
just above the surface to land in a long line
as if posing for a family photo.

First one, then another and another,
flap their wings, raise fountains of water,
soak themselves and splash the gulls nearby.
Utter delight—everyone getting along.

THE PLACE YOU'D CALL HOME

for Hillary LeClaire, USMC

Walking to White Pond, I often pause
to lean a while against the chain link fence
at the airport in Chatham and wait for
planes to land, their wings dipping left and right
as they skim the treetops, cut their speed,
and cruise towards the single runway.
I think of the gulls I'll see soon, performing
the same feat at the pond, but with more
finesse and grace than any pilot but you,
my friend. You could land as smoothly as
the gulls, yet were happiest when sky bound,
flying high. Coming back, I rest on the bench
we installed in your memory at the airfield,
the place you'd dock your plane and call home.

CRANBERRY FIELDS FOREVER

On one of my daily walks last autumn,
I found myself bogged down again,
wandering alone without direction or
purpose in an early morning fog
that augured a splendid day in my world
if not that of many others, and yet I
could not feel the promise of something
new until I happened upon a sign

NO TRESPASSING
THIS IS A WORKING FARM

Scanning for some authority figure
who might shoo me away, I stepped past
the warning and moved to the bog's
edge, where I took off shoes and socks,
slid out of jeans and shirt down to
boxers, waded in and swished forward
to waist deep, my feet sinking into
the mush. Closing my eyes, I stretched
my arms and legs, lay back and floated
among the cranberries, bright red and
ready for harvest. Later, when I could
feel the sun, I opened my eyes wide
to the cloud-free blue, the mist having
burned away. Everything seemed right.

Ripples in the Fabric of the Universe

The conditions are right—a cloudless dome
not cluttered with pinpricks of light, dusk still
collecting itself into night. A view
clear to the horizon, my gaze a full
sweep of one-hundred-and-eighty degrees.
Overhead, the Summer Triangle as
sharp as I've ever found it. To the south,
Jupiter, Saturn, and Mars are aligned,
maybe an omen that the unrest growing
in the world might play itself out before
its tidal waves sweep away everything
we hold dear. In the grand scheme of things,
they're mere ripples in the fabric of the
universe, but not to us here on Earth.

BIOGRAPHICAL NOTE

Jim Tilley has published three full-length collections of poetry, *In Confidence*, *Cruising at Sixty to Seventy*, *Lessons from Summer Camp*, and a novel, *Against the Wind*, with Red Hen Press. His short memoir, *The Elegant Solution*, was published as a Ploughshares Solo. He won *Sycamore Review*'s Wabash Prize for Poetry for "The Art of Patience."